HERE WE GO DIGGING FOR DINOSAUR BONES

SUNG TO THE TUNE OF "HERE WE GO 'ROUND THE MULBERRY BUSH"

SUSAN LENDROTH

Illustrated by **BOB KOLAR**

ini Charlesbridge

HERE WE GO DIGGING for dinosaur bones,

dinosaur bones,

dinosaur bones.

Here we go digging for dinosaur bones
on a warm and sunny morning.

Many people, from workers constructing a new
building to children playing in a field, have found
dinosaur bones by accident. But scientists travel
all over the world to the places they think
offer the best chance of finding fossils.

This is the way we hike the trail,

hike the trail,

hike the trail.

This is the way we hike the trail on a warm and sunny morning.

Fossils are the remains of animals and plants that died long ago. Paleontologists are scientists who study fossils. They hunt for them in areas where rocks formed millions of years ago.

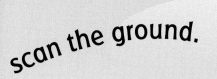

scan the ground.

This is the way we scan the ground
on a warm and sunny morning.

Sometimes, when a dinosaur died,
mud or sand quickly covered its body.
Over time the body decomposed, leaving
behind just the skeleton. Minerals slowly
replaced the bones, creating fossils.

This is the way we excavate, excavate, excavate.

This is the way we excavate on a warm and sunny morning.

When paleontologists find a dinosaur fossil, they dig around it to look for more pieces of the dinosaur. They also may find fossils of plants and other animals from the same time period.

This is the way we sift through dirt,

sift through dirt,

sift through dirt. **This is the way we sift through dirt on a warm and sunny morning.**

Fossils can be as big as a refrigerator or as small as a grain of sand. To build a dinosaur skeleton, paleontologists want to find every scrap available. They sift dirt through wire screens to find the teeny-tiny bits.

This is the way we wrap our finds,

wrap our finds,

wrap our finds.

This is the way we wrap our finds
on a warm and sunny morning.

Sometimes it's safer to leave a large fossil in a
surrounding block of stone and to lift it out as one large
piece. Paleontologists wrap the block in cloth, paper
towels, or even toilet paper. They then cover it with a
hard layer of plaster to protect it during transportation.

clean the bones. This is the way we clean the bones on a warm and sunny morning.

Back in the laboratory, scientists and technicians carefully clean each fossil. They use chemicals, chisels, brushes, and the picks your dentist uses on your teeth.

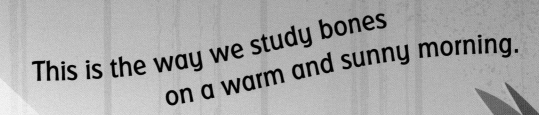

This is the way we study bones
on a warm and sunny morning.

Dinosaurs lived millions of years ago, but we have a good idea of what they looked like from their fossils. Paleontologists study fossilized bones like a jigsaw puzzle to decide what goes where when building a dinosaur skeleton.

This is the way we bu___ T. rex,

build T. rex,

_____ T. rex.

This is the way we build *T. rex* on a warm and sunny morning.

Most fossil skeletons are not complete when they are found. Paleontologists figure out what the missing parts should be and make models of them. All the pieces, both the fossils and the reproductions, are fitted together on a metal frame to build a dinosaur skeleton.

This is the way it bares its teeth
on a warm and sunny morning.

T. Rex had more than fifty large teeth in its massive jaws, some up to a foot long. Scientists think it may have had the most powerful bite of any land animal ever.

Let's go digging for dinosaur bones,
dinosaur bones,
dinosaur bones.

Let's go digging for dinosaur bones
on a warm and sunny morning.

Fossils can be found in many places, and anyone can hunt for them, even kids. What dinosaurs would you like to find?

DINOS AND FOSSILS AND BIRDS, OH MY!

STEGOSAURUS

TYRANNOSAURUS REX

PATAGOTITAN

Dinosaurs walked the earth for more than 180 million years, but not all types of dinosaurs lived at the same time. For example, tens of millions of years passed between the era of the *Stegosaurus* and that of *Tyrannosaurus rex*. By comparison, modern humans, *Homo sapiens*, have existed for about two hundred thousand years.

Dinosaurs came in many shapes and sizes. *Compsognathus* was as small as a chicken. One of the largest dinosaurs, *Patagotitan*, weighed in at nearly 70 tons—heavier than ten African elephants! New dinosaur species are still being discovered, so one day someone—perhaps you—may find one that's even larger.

People have been finding fossils for thousands of years, but scientists did not realize that these were from prehistoric animals until the 1800s. Paleontologists have discovered not only fossilized bones and teeth, but also the remains of dinosaur eggs, skin, feathers, footprints, and even poop. All these fossils give clues to how dinosaurs looked and lived, but new discoveries constantly change our understanding. For example, researchers now think many (perhaps most) dinosaurs had feathers, even though they did not fly.

COMPSOGNATHUS

SPARROW

Scientists believe a large asteroid impacted Earth sixty-five million years ago, leading to the extinction of the dinosaurs. Not all dinosaurs died at that time, though. A few survived to evolve into the birds we know today. When you see sparrows hopping on the ground or a hawk soaring with the wind, you are looking at descendants of the dinosaurs.

READ, SING, AND DIG!

Paleontologists hike, dig, and build. You can, too!
Act out the story as you sing along with the book.

This is the way we **HIKE** the trail: Swing your arms back and forth as though walking with a purpose.

SCAN the ground: Put a hand above your eyes and search the room.

EXCAVATE: Dig with your invisible shovel.

SIFT through dirt: Imagine holding a tray between your hands and shaking it back and forth.

WRAP our finds: Pretend you are winding a bandage around your arm.

CLEAN the bones: Cup one hand and use the other as a scrub brush.

STUDY bones: Curl both hands into tubes to form a microscope and peer through it.

BUILD *T. Rex*: Stack your fists higher and higher.

And everyone can **BARE** their teeth
and chomp like a dinosaur!

The illustrations for this story are set in Montana's Hell Creek Formation, a well-known site for fossil digs. Scattered through the art are some of the critters that live in that area today. Can you find them?

WESTERN TANAGER

WESTERN MEADOWLARK

GREATER SHORT-HORNED LIZARD

RED-WINGED BLACKBIRD

PLAINS SPADEFOOT TOAD

WESTERN MILK SNAKE

To my old friends Susan (Getz) Lyon and Denise
(Woo) Seymour: Sue, Sue, and Woo forever!
(And I'm not saying we're dinosaurs.)—**S. L.**

For Everett—**B. K.**

Special thanks to Alan Zdinak, fossil preparator at the Natural History Museum of
Los Angeles County, and Carol J. Stadum, associate in the paleontology department
at the San Diego Natural History Museum, for their invaluable advice and expertise.

Text copyright © 2020 by Susan Lendroth
Illustrations copyright © 2020 by Bob Kolar
All rights reserved, including the right of reproduction in
whole or in part in any form. Charlesbridge and colophon
are registered trademarks of Charlesbridge Publishing, Inc.

Published by Charlesbridge
85 Main Street, Watertown, MA 02472
(617) 926-0329 • www.charlesbridge.com

Printed in China
(hc) 10 9 8 7 6 5 4 3 2 1

Artwork was created with a computer using lots of pixels
    (no dinosaurs were harmed in the creation of this book)
Display type set in Manihot by PintassilgoPrints
Text type set in Badger by Red Rooster Collection
Color separations by Colourscan Print Co Pte Ltd.
    in Singapore
Printed by 1010 Printing International Limited
    in Huizhou, Guangdong, China
Production supervision by Brian G. Walker
Designed by Sarah Richards Taylor

Library of Congress Cataloging-in-Publication Data
Names: Lendroth, Susan, author. | Kolar, Bob, illustrator.
Title: Here we go digging for dinosaur bones:
    (sung to the tune of "here we go round the mulberry
    bush") / by Susan Lendroth; illustrated by Bob Kolar.
Description: Watertown, MA: Charlesbridge, [2020]
Identifiers: LCCN 2018032573 (print) |
    LCCN 2018035528 (ebook) |
    ISBN 9781632898685 (ebook) |
    ISBN 9781632898692 (ebook pdf) |
    ISBN 9781623541040 (reinforced for library use)
Subjects: LCSH: Dinosaurs—Juvenile literature. |
    Paleontology—Juvenile literature. |
    Fossils—Juvenile literature. | Children's songs—Texts.
Classification: LCC QE861.4 (ebook) | LCC QE861.4 .L45
    2019 (print) | DDC 567.9—dc23
LC record available at https://lccn.loc.gov/2018032573

At the time of publication, any URLs printed in this
book were accurate and active. Charlesbridge, the author,
and the illustrator are not responsible for the content
or accessibility of any URL.